The Khristos Cantos

poems by

Michael E. Williams

Finishing Line Press
Georgetown, Kentucky

The Khristos Cantos

Copyright © 2017 by Michael Williams
ISBN 978-1-63534-373-1 First Edition
All rights reserved under International and Pan-American Copyright Conventions. No part of this book may be reproduced in any manner whatsoever without written permission from the publisher, except in the case of brief quotations embodied in critical articles and reviews.

ACKNOWLEDGMENTS

For all those who have been the Word made flesh for me.

Publisher: Leah Maines

Editor: Christen Kincaid

Cover Art: Ed Batsel

Author Photo: Peggy I Sewell

Cover Design: Elizabeth Maines McCleavy

Printed in the USA on acid-free paper.
Order online: www.finishinglinepress.com
              also available on amazon.com

Author inquiries and mail orders:
Finishing Line Press
P. O. Box 1626
Georgetown, Kentucky 40324
U. S. A.

Table of Contents

The Spikes 1
The Spikes #2 2
The Mallets Fall 3
Swinging Mallets 4
Soldiers Strut 5
The Place of the Skull 6
A Thousand Bone-Hard Voices 7
Bodies Writhe 8
Prepare 9
Prepare #2 10
The Spike Is Set 11
Prepare #3 12
Across the Desert 13
Baptissimo 14
Temptatio 15
The Raising of the Tree 16
A Plain Sermon 17
A Merchant's Price 20
The Drink 21
Supper 22
The Donkey's Back 23
In Another Garden 24
Let It Pass 25
A Final Word 26
Epilogue of Sorts 27

1 The Spikes

Spack
Spack
Spack
Spack
Spack
Spack
Spack
Spack

Clack
Clack
   Clack
      Clack
         Clack
            Clack
               Clack

3 The Mallets Fall

the mallets fall

clack, spack
spike points tear
flesh between
wrist bones

spack, clack
in time
to no time

4 Swinging Mallets

swinging mallets
ringing spike heads
mark the time
of breath left
time to end
all time

5 Soldiers Strut

soldiers strut
crimson cloaks
armor gleaming
ornamental birds
cackles and guffaws
pierce the hearing
of mothers, sisters, wives
here to watch
sons, brothers, husbands
die

6 The Place of the Skull

this is the place
the place, the place of the skull
the place of justice, retribution
this is the place
the place, the place of the skull
the place of deaths
of final breaths
this is the place
the place, the place of the skull

7 A Thousand Bone-Hard Voices

a thousand bone-hard voices
echo through the burning brains
of those who hang
pull…inhale
release…exhale
anger, desolation
of the dying
laughter, exaltation
of the skull

8 Bodies Writhe

bodies writhe
pinned against the sky
a butterfly collection
of shattered voices
the slightest breath
settling like dust
upon the city below

9 Prepare

once there was
a word
a voice
in the desert
one who came
in skins
cried, "Prepare!
one who came fasting
cried, "Prepare!"
one who came baptizing cried, "Prepare!"
prepare the way
the way of the word
prepare the way of the word
make straight the highway
for the breath of God

10 Prepare #2

one who came from Nazareth
heard, "Prepare!"
the one who came eating and drinking
heard, "Prepare!"
the one who came to the waters
heard, "Prepare!"
prepare the way of the word
make straight the highway
for the breath of God

11 The Spike Is Set

the spike is set
predicts another death to come
then another
almost too far away to hear
the world is encrusted
with incessant voices
is there no word whispered into the world
wrapped in laughter
transported to this place
of cries and groaning
from a world beyond voices

12 Prepare #3

once there was
a word
a voice
crying in the desert
Prepare
the one who came in skins cried
Prepare
The one who came fasting cried
Prepare
the one who came baptizing cried
Prepare
prepare the way
the way of the lord
prepare the way of the lord
john ben zechariah cried
make straight the highway for our God.
the one who came from Nazareth heard
Prepare
the one who came in carpenter's tunic heard
Prepare
the one who came eating and drinking heard
Prepare
the one who came to be baptized heard
Prepare
prepare the way
the way of the lord
prepare the way
of the lord
joshua ben joseph heard
make straight the highway for our God.

13 Across the Desert

the hot winds shift the sanded face
of an earth infertile and arid
the corpses of stunted bushes
        wheel like drunken zombies
twisting along their inscrutable paths
        whose destination only the wind knows

the horizon is the delicious fulcrum of the sky
        we lift the sands and winds
            with our glance
        toward the vortex of suns
at evening a remnant of wilderness light
        stretches like a tired refugee
            upon the gritty pallet of endings

14 Baptissimo

morning enters quietly on bird feet
                gently drawing breath
from the fevered earth
                offering moist health
to sustain the humid longing
                on its journey to the river

the river is chill
a strand of relief in a world on fire
this is the place of the voice
                drawing like a magnet
                      the fragments
of our shattered
                adolescent world

the voice walks in skins
                the unwashed cleanser
the wild-haired locust eating voice
proclaiming in the desert
marking the campaign trail
                of the incumbent kingdom
that was and is and shall be evermore

the ear-stopping water
                shuts out differentiated sound
immersed in the oblivion
            of the one
                    undivided
                                  self
arising from the river
                slapped by the sun
                      into breath
the carpenter's laughter
                flitters like a flock of birds
                            enough to fill a thousand heavens

15 Temptatio

the return was long
      the ascetic wanderer
            fasting
    in the desert
        visions
    are conjured
from evening's atmosphere
      stones become bread
           before hungry eyes
sand hills stand like temples
      with great difficulty
               the traveler
holds himself back
      keeps himself from hurling
           down the long bank
into a world
      beyond sun and sand

after forty days and nights
      of cacophonous voices
           offering gifts from
                the weary earth
the wanderer blinks to clear
      dust clouded eyes
           he marches surrounded
by the mercenary armies of the earth
      he mutters beneath labored breaths
           his inscrutable syllables
                to the sky

16 The Raising of the Tree

    the Khristos' eyes are captured by the sky
        moving like planets across the liquid
            shifting landscape
    across the elongated torsos of soldiers
        standing over him
            mallets in hand
                raised to strike
                      and strike they do
    "bring him up" so many voices
    ascetics, soldiers, women
        the carpenter laughs
            it is laughable
        to be finished by the fruits
            of one's own trade

    the wooden crossbar creaks
        as its stem is planted in the hole
    the loose dirt shudders beneath the weight
        of the tree of death
            sporting its sordid fruit

    the final setting is a sharp and painful jolt
        suddenly the sky is stolen
            and the eyes of the Khristos
    settle on the clusters of humanity
        clinging for life to the flat earth
    wants to speak but the time for words
        is hidden in distant mountains
            the way to which is forgotten

17 A Plain Sermon

the hearers sat as if they could not move
those who were drunk shattered the silence with shouts
their mistresses chattered like small animals
old women spat through gaps left by missing teeth
would the carpenter be able to force his voice
        beyond the length of his arm
"are you poor?" laughter
        the answer was obvious
"what do you have?"
        shouts carried like storms across the water
" nothing"
            "wrong!
you are blessed above all the rest
        yours is the kingdom of heaven"
"you can't eat the kingdom of heaven, preacher!"
        "are you hungry, then?
sometimes words strike too close to the heart
        "don't waste our time with questions
you already know the answer to"
        "then you shall have your fill
and your children their fill
        go ahead, weep for yourselves
and your children
        for one day you will laugh, believe me,
and your laughter will fill the cities
        and the deserts and the mountains
it will drown the clatter of money
        and overcome the voices of death."
some began to leave grumbling at his words
        "this is crazy talk, this is madness!"
"that's what others will say of you is you repeat my words
        but don't let that trouble you
when people call my words crazy, call you mad
        kick you   spit on you

consider it their blessing upon you
        didn't they do the same
to the prophets?
        look with pity upon the wealthy
they are satisfied with what they have
        that is all they will receive
look with pity upon those with full bellies
        one day hunger will be their companion
and they won't know what to do
        look with pity with those who bathe in the praise of others
that is the sure sign of a false prophet
        tell me, how many of you have been kicked
or spat upon or beaten or robbed?
        do the people who afflict you love you?"
heads move from side to side
        where could this line of reasoning
possibly lead?
        "love them instead
whoever strikes you like a slave
        turn your other cheek and say
strike me like an equal
        whatever someone takes from you offer more
even those who live by violence and theft
        need to know love
before they too can love.
        if you love expecting to be loved
whose interest do you have at heart?
        your own or the person
who needed to be loved?
        anyone can love those who love them back
if you want to love like God loves
        love your enemies
do your best for those
        who only wish the worst for you

don't be loan sharks of love
        the crowd had dwindled
men took the arms of their mistresses
        walked back toward town
playfully noting one word—love—
        they went to explore its possibilities
others muttered against their licentiousness
        their lack of faith
"have you missed the point of all I have said?"
        the Khristos asked
"I know how you love to sit in the judge's seat
        it's this simple
don't judge and you won't be judged
        don't you see that you will be judged by the rules you write
in judgment of others?
        your job is to forgive
you know enough for that
        only God knows enough to judge

18 A Merchant's Price

does God exact a merchant's price
    or hawk his wares in the street?
is our God a moneychanger?
    God doesn't hoard minutes like money
the creator will not splinter the creation
    a tree grows in the forest
    straight
    tall
    silent
in the fullness of its seasons
    we hew the tree and plane it for our uses
this is not God's doing
    to God all time is one time
we think we run out of time
    only then do we truly see God
tell me this, what would you say
if a farmer hired you in the morning
to work in his vineyard
at noon he hired more workers
at evening even more
yet when the wages are paid
all are paid the same?
such are the wages of the kingdom of heaven

19 The Drink

the wine had soured
      like words too long held in the heart
held in the mouth, words that melt over withered lips
      "God how can you leave me
at such a time as this?"

20 Supper

I have known sweet wine
        good bread
"do this"
"every time?"
"remembrance"
"do this"
"remembrance"
"do this"
"every time?"
"do this"

21 TheDonkey's Back

      the donkey's back is bony
this forty dollar beast of burden
      all these people
all this shouting
      the furor that precedes
the final word

22 In Another Garden

after rain
inhale the intimate odor
of the earth
the evening
it's iridescent glow
peculiar to the day's departure
after rain
everything is gray/green
the color whose last word
is darkness

23 Let It Pass

      God, let it pass
even at this last hour
can it be too late
to take up another trade
another venture
or return to the builder's mallet?

      God, let it pass
all this and you exact more
did any prophet do as much?
even now it's not too late

      God let it pass
the others sleep
the wicked prosper
they drink the sweet draught
why did you save the dregs for me?

      yet if no other food
will satisfy their hunger
assuage their thirst
wipe their slates clean
then let my body be that food
my blood that drink
      thy will not mine

      the mallet has passed from my hand
to theirs
      thy will not mine
      drive the spikes quickly
there is no stopping now
      drive them quickly home

23 A Final Word

Finished!
Finished!
Finished!
Finished!
Finished!
Finished!
Finished!
Finished!

24 Epilogue (of sorts)

all that has been
and all that will ever be
is one with all that is
tellers of tales
weave the wistful strands
of memory and imagination
into a web of wonder
the word has taken on the garments of the world
only to have them ripped off
the flesh was too close, too real,
so flesh is turned back into words
bake the sweet bread that passes for faith
go ahead and taste it
but never for a moment
pretend that it could ever be
the bitter morsel that was God's

Michael Williams was born in Murray, Kentucky and has spent most of his life in Tennessee. He was educated at Vanderbilt University, Garrett-Evangelical Theological Seminary, and holds a PhD from Northwestern University.

Michael is a United Methodist pastor, who has lectured at Princeton Theological Seminary, Emmanuel College of The University of Toronto, Morehead State University, and at a number of other colleges and universities.

He has been a featured teller at the National Storytelling Festival in Jonesborough, Tennessee, and has taught workshops on writing and storytelling across the country and has been publishing for over four decades.

He is the author or editor of twenty non-fiction books, and has written three plays that have been produced. His poetry has appeared in *The Southern Poetry Review, Appalachian Heritage, Southern Humanities Review, Cold Mountain Review, Still, The Pikeville Review*, and other journals. His work has been nominated for a Pushcart Prize. While he was a student a collection of his poems was awarded the Academy of American Poets Prize at Northwestern University.

His most recent books are *Take Nothing for Your Journey* published by Finishing Line Press (2016) and *Spoken into Being: Divine Encounters through Story* from Upper Room Books (2017). He lives in Nashville, Tennessee and serves as Writer/Storyteller-in-Residence at Martin Methodist College.

www.ingramcontent.com/pod-product-compliance
Lightning Source LLC
LaVergne TN
LVHW041517070426
835507LV00012B/1645